CUICACALLI / HOUSE OF SONG

CUICACALLI / HOUSE OF SONG

ire'ne lara silva

SADDLE ROAD PRESS

Cuicacalli / House of Song
© 2019 Ire'ne Lara Silva

Saddle Road Press
Hilo, Hawai'i
saddleroadpress.com

Cover art ("Bloodsong") by Moisés S. L. Lara
Cover and book design by Don Mitchell

ISBN 978-1-7329521-1-9

Tambien de dolor se canta,
cuando llorar no se puede.

Quien canta,
sus males espanta.

—Popular Dichos Mexicanos

Dedicated to Moisés, for surviving everything that came...

to a loved community of friends and strangers
that kept us afloat in a time of crisis...

and to the memory of my mother, who believed
it was a spiritual commandment to be brave...
los valientes, *she'd say,* no se dan por vencidos.

Contents

A Hundred Hands Deep

What Else Do We Burn

Cuicacalli

Afterword

A Hundred Hands Deep

you love a river

for twenty years you love a river   and every time you
cross it or sit to stare at it   you imagine your suddenly
immense hands brushing over its calm ripples   as if it
was fur   as if it was skin   as if it could touch
you back   as if it also loved you   as if it had
waited for you always   this peaceful uncontested
river   always serene   so different from that other
river   the river that has defined your entire life

the river you love is far but not that far   from that other
river   that other river sometimes muddy   sometimes
dry   sometimes green   sometimes lovely but you can
never think of it without seeing almost two centuries of
blood shed over it   can never see it   without
thinking of the lives   the pain   the hurt   the
losses   crossing that river has cost   you have always
loved rivers   but is it still a river   if it has walls

poem for Tlaltecuhtli

diosa
                    this is the long arrived at truth   you reveal
we birth ourselves   and we birth ourselves
        the new self   readying itself   to give birth
        as soon as it is born   as soon as it is strong enough
to squat on its haunches   with gritted teeth
        eyes gone half-mad with pain
eyes gone half-blind with awe   an ouroboros of
beings   squatting on their haunches   with gritted
teeth   shoulders braced   and eyes gone half-
mad with pain   eyes gone half-blind with awe
        screaming infinity with one throat because
        endlessly   we are both being born
        and giving birth

not woman body   not man body   not human
body   body of light   body of sound   body
of earth   body of flesh entrusted   with
the names of stars   entrusted with the raw stuff of
creation   body of bone and blood
            entrusted with that which   visions
                    body of death and birth   entrusted with
carrying all songs   entrusted with the singing itself

                                            divina
we will remember what has been forgotten   remember
what has never been forgotten   live in that which
never leaves us   labor as you labor
        birthing ourselves   birthing
        birthing   for everything that dies
this is the wholeness we are   the infinity we are

walking the chupacabra

for Deborah Miranda

every morning we put the leash around his rough furred neck let him take the lead out the door and onto the sidewalk while the neighbors look askance at us we walk the chupacabra every morning or shall we say he consents to let us walk him and we walk on the balls of our feet here we are walking the chupacabra or shall we say walking the threat of violence walking the shadow of imminent death we walk on the balls of our feet and breathe rapidly ready to run should he decide to turn and maul us should he become unable to hold his hunger in check not hunger for flesh but hunger to see life spilled life burst life ended

we walk the chupacabra praying under our breaths hesitating when he stops to inspect a bush or a butterfly or a dog walking down the opposite side of the street we never hesitate when he decides to change direction we speed our steps almost trip over ourselves we walk the chupacabra or shall we say we walk danger incarnated walk rage concentrated in a four-legged form we turn back when and only when his eyes turn homewards and his horns cast shadows he waits while we open the lock on the door while we remove the leash while we pour water into his bowl and use a knife on our hands to add enough of our blood so that he'll always recognize us we do not serve him anything to eat we still don't know what he eats he has no bed sometimes we find him asleep on the ceiling

at night we sleep in this house this house where the chupacabra sleeps we sleep with our eyes open in case he wakes we sleep in this house which always smells slightly of blood and smoke of wild things of anguish not anguish and hunger not hunger of remembrance always remembrance of vengeance desperately seeking to name itself something else we live we sleep we eat we love we make things in this house where the chupacabra lives this house guarded by the chupacabra

15

We Played Survival

Our game had no other name. Find shelter.
The picnic table became the roof of our
home. Find food. The long grass with its
seed-heavy tips became our corn. We stalked
the bob white quails. With stealth, with
quickness, with hunger in our eyes, we
trapped them. We always released them, but
the important thing was to catch them.
Catching them meant that even in our
imagination, hunger lost its sharpness. We
built a fire against the winter cold. Gathered
kindling. Stacked firewood. We read the sky
and the sun.

Listened and heard unknown voices on the
wind. Someone had to stand guard. We
needed weapons. I don't remember if we
whispered the dangers or only moved as one
to do what was needed. They would not burn
our home. They would not shoot us. They
would not slit our throats. They would not
take us alive.

I was seven years old. My brother five. We
played in utter silence. No shouting. No
laughing. Nothing done carelessly. What did
we know of history. What memories lived in
our bones.

i like the words on my skin

words meant for me first   making my skin into paper
    like the blank page before words   like the
page overflowing with words   like a page of poetry
    half ink   half white space

weren't they there always   waiting to emerge
from beneath   my skin   not the needle
injecting ink   but the needle piercing the skin
    releasing the ink

you will not persuade me   that sometimes it isn't
    blood   that runs in my veins
what else is like this   mine before it was mine
    waiting for me only

no one else will see   these writhing lines of black
and red   symbols from all my languages
    moving like twisting serpents   across my skin

bursting like riotously   blooming vines
    exploding with green leaves   each leaf
holding   within it   a breath

i trace each line   my fingers   come away dripping
ink   i bring my hands to my mouth   ink
enough   to transform   breath into words

when i am gone   this is what will remain of me
    everything i couldn't contain   spiraling
galaxies of ink   everything i fought   to give

Coatlicue

i am not your broken daughter healing and breaking in turns i've
spent my life with your other faces a pantheon of feminine gods
learning the lessons of humility and endurance sacrifice and patience
    i've known your name all my life your name and the name
    they said was yours softening all the hard consonants of
    you to fashion something softer to their foreign tongues
your image was always there even for me born north of the river to
parents born north of the river but my eyes never rested on you
never traced your image until i left the lands of my childhood
    you lived in me but i shied away took refuge in turquoise
    and roses and stars in dark skin and powder blue robes in
    the round mother the gentle mother the earth mother
but the years came for me and death came for me and loss came for
me and how many times now have i grown new hearts and then they
came for my head and what was left but to follow your example
    i look in the mirror and see you you are in my bones two
    snake heads emerging from my neck serpent skin over my
    face serpent eyes and serpent fangs and i keep surviving
at 43 now i say your name in my sleep at 43 i crave the sight of you
and keep your image close at 43 i can rest with your serpent heads and
severed hands and anguished hearts i carry skulls of my own now
    we cast identical shadows and when the sun shines in my
    eyes i see the stone of you i see what i could not see before
    you have always been the one beneath above beyond
i have lived waiting to arrive at you waiting to return to you my
blood hums here near you and you are silent because near you words
begin to collapse and all i do is speak and speak and speak
    but near you all measures of beauty all measures of terror fail
    everything strong and everything implacable gathers living
    dying living in turn and your silence your silence fills me

what i remembered yesterday

at 6, i was the loner kid. the migrant kid following harvest
seasons in texas, oklahoma, new mexico. we moved every few months,
changing schools, changing homes. i was the poor kid. the dark
brown kid. the only girl with short short hair and pants.

i was the quiet kid who stared at clouds and blades of grass. who
walked the perimeter of the schoolyard as if plotting escape. a
child in pain with no words for that pain.

iliana was one of the pretty girls. the girls who would grow up to
become cheerleaders. iliana with the pretty gold skin only slightly
lighter than her light brown hair. iliana with eyes blacker than
mine. i don't know what she did or said, but one day the
cheerleaders-to-be sent her sprawling into the dirt and turned away.

i don't remember if i helped her, or if, finding herself alone, she
sought me out. but from one moment to another, i went from alone
to not-alone. impossible that we had ever been apart.

little soulmate. mirror reflection. inseparable. we had one shadow.
we spent every second of her exile breathing the same air. staring
at the same clouds. holding the same wildflowers. she held my
hand.

i loved her with all the passion of my 6 year old heart. that should
be funny, but it isn't. because the passion of my 6 year old heart
was not the passion of my 17 year old heart or my 21 year old
heart or my heart at any other point.

at 6, a heart is infinite. devoid of want. devoid of selfishness.
devoid of games. devoid of possession. devoid of armor. at 6, a
heart is infinite.

i don't remember time. was it weeks? months? i only remember i had no warning. one day to the next, her exile ended. the cheerleaders-to-be took her back. i waited for her but she never returned to our meeting place. i watched to see if she'd turn and catch my eye and smile her quiet smile but she never did.

almost 40 years later, i wonder, did it begin then? this lifelong love of heartbreak songs. betrayal songs. abandonment songs. unrequited songs. my 6 year old voice didn't know the songs i would learn later.

maybe i was 15 or 16 or 17 when *that* song found me. the song i didn't know would follow me always. the song i know no matter how many years pass without singing it. the song i've known late, early, tired, drunk, sober, heart silent and heart pealing.

probablemente ya, de mi te has olvidado
*y mientras tanto yo, te seguire esperando**

yesterday i remembered the 6 year old me. and my 6 year old heart. and i remembered what i'd forgotten — the 6 year old lives in me still. the 6 year old in me that waits and waits and is still waiting.

*"Se Me Olvido Otra Vez" by Juan Gabriel

sometimes i crave the color red

the way others crave
red-bleeding fruit or a mouth to bruise with tenderness
or a scrap of silk stretched taut
                                            i
                                crave the color red
and scrape my teeth on my bottom lip crave the color red
and test the air with flared nostrils crave the color red
and clench my own thighs to keep from reaching out
            blindly madly hungrily
                                        in every direction
this craving for red is
                        welcome
                                        there were years i forgot the
color red years i forgot to want it years i forgot wanting to want

you'd think that desire
        left abandoned rusting? would lose its memories
of sharp and of shining and of shamelessness but no
not so

        i might have said   then   that desire was a knife desire
        was madness impulse need   desire was a gnawing ache

        that desire like youthful beauty now seems a thing skin
deep to what this is
            heat radiating from the bone making my heart a
crouching lion
            desire now is articulation desire now knows   death
        and cages everything that is bitter and   everything that is
        sweet

and i know no other name for this now   this
                                              illumination
                                              within

it seems to me the stars are enduring

here where i stand the ancestors stood. the same wind. the same
night sky. the same trees. the same sweet scent of grass. i
touch my face and the hand touching my face is a
hundred hands deep.

we are like lost children who do not know our birth names. do not know
our birth mothers. as if we had been taken. as if we
had been abandoned. as if we had been raised in a
world without mirrors.

the world confuses history with truth. victims with survivors. lines on a
map for reality. the headlines proclaim us foreign,
dangerous and dark-skinned hordes invading what
has never existed.

this is my earth. not theirs. it has always been my earth. taste it and my
blood and your tongue will confuse the two. the
one. this sky and my spirit. also one. the same
ardent shade of blue.

and this is my face. my face as it has been for a thousand years all my
mothers' faces. i walk the same steps listening to a
half-song, dreaming a half-song. my voice fashions
a half-song.

but my hands are not half-hands. my heart is not a half-heart. my blood is
not half-blood. my soul is not half-soul.
if i stand they stand. if i live they live. if i
breathe they breathe.

if i speak they speak through me. if i heal they heal through me. i am never
alone. i am never only one. i am the embodiment of
a thousand years' desire to survive.
to live. to be. free.

here where i stand the ancestors stood. the same wind. the same night sky.
the same trees. the same sweet scent of grass. i
touch my face and the hand touching my face is a
hundred hands deep.

it seems to me the stars are enduring.

let the constellations in

i. i wanted to be alone

                    but not in my bed. i
wanted my womb to lie fallow and fertile,
wanted to choose different birthings.
different creatings. but now my arms ache
for their sweet weight. where are my
children.
                    where are my loves.
what was sweet. i forgot the sweet. i've
detonated my memories. have i forgotten
you too. i knew your name.
                    crushed pomegranate
on my eyes. dark river currents.

the animals in their burrows howled.
                    splintered stars.
rivers of stars overhead and the weight of
the moonlight. resistance of ocean heaving
against my hands. purple clouds on the
horizon.

                    black ocean. it could
wash us away — me and the thought of you i
carry. exquisite burden. a lover's weight on
a woman's body. black ocean. white lines of
foam. ocean bed beneath my feet. saltwater
against my thighs. the tides are chiseling me
into being. a woman shaped boulder
                    ebb and flow. grains
of salt scouring away all roughness. ebb and

flow. white crests of waves falling in
benedictions. outstretched arms and raised
face. black ocean. adore this

ii. what if the road led us away from its light

                what if i called out
wanting to touch your hands and you turned
and i didn't recognize you. even your scent
unknowable.
                the night sky says
stop. the darkness bursts at its center seam.

not all dreaming is true.
                i would have slept but
there were voices drifting in my
bloodstream. the night had too much to say.
                i never closed the
door. the wind took up residence inside me.
swirling and howling. restless. climbing
whirling exulting shrieking whispering
inside me. i took up residence in the wind,
limbs flailing contentedly. glowing eyes
spinning. healing uncontrollably.
                both of us howling
like animals. animals in rhythms of
surviving. animals in rhythms of
luminescence. bliss. dissolution.

iii. unchain the animals

                let them run while the
sun is still high. let them run. give them

earth. give them sky. and no more than what
hunger demands.

there have been no
words or too many words choking strangling
twisting snapping the raw grating of teeth on
bone bodies were not meant to live in flight
in free fall but holding close to other human
hands the warmth of other bodies we would
forget we were alive we would forget we
could die your breath what is mine but the
luxury of a lack of hostages too many words
obscuring compassion strangling peace too
many corrosive words too many words these
are just more too many words i want them to
collapse too many words the healing lies
beneath beyond between them there have
been no words soft enough

my face disfigured by
words. i burned the ashes. i burned the earth.
i burned the palms of my hands. i ate the
smoke. keeping the fire lit took my
everything. one breath at a time. my body
my hands my eyes feeding the embers.

iv. i came to dance, i said

i came to dance. on
the naked earth always with my naked feet. i
danced under stars. how many nights have i
watched those bodies, those animal clouds,
running across the night sky. half song and
half raw heat. immense stampedes. neighing.

hooves wisping into black smoke. heaving.
rolling.

body, when did you
ever move to the demands of joy and not the
necessities of rage. only when you were
dancing, body, and only when you were
alone.

i wanted to be as
alone as i felt. to drink in aloneness with my
skin. eat it with my eyes. i held my
aloneness close. murmured endearments.
kissed it. cursed it.

diagram my soul,
hands. dissect it layer by layer: the gardens
of butterflies and black-winged crows, the
soft scrapings of dried rose petals and paper,
the blue pools of sorrow i kept close to the
song'd canyons, the vast fields of tilled
black earth, the silvered prairies burning.

map my soul. draw
black lines on my hands so i won't forget. so
i won't lose my way on a dark day. a dark
year. a dark decade.

v. shadow what is your name

shadow why are you
here shadow why won't you let me sleep
shadow why do you follow me your
gleaming eyes peering at me from behind
the door shadow why the shifting faces why

the whimpering of a wounded animal
shadow i know you have no face
                        futile to fear i will
regret my spent life. what difference is there
between what i chose and what chose me.
flourishing, fracturing, seeking, escaping.
we return always to ourselves.
                        hoping our arms are
open. hoping our eyes are open.
                        you birth yourself.
you birth yourself. you birth yourself. you
birth yourself. again. again. again. this is
what time teaches you.
                        time collapses was are
will be would have been what you forgot
what you will never forget is collapse
infinity is infinity another way of breathing
touch time sometimes you can see it silver
viscous and silver

vi. this is not the story

                        not the language. not
the sound. unsay unmake unseam unspeak
undo. burn it all.
                        i lost no one. no one
lost me. we are animals. walking and
breathing in the barbarous ways of hermits.
am i still following you. are you still there.
                        what is this. memory
and not memory. dream and prediction.

everything that collapses. green shoots in the
black soil. small fists, anxious to birth.
gnawing solidities, creating fissures to let
the constellations in. light streaming in
where there were wounds. we hold night. we
hold stars. the story tells us everything. tells
us nothing. the story doesn't begin again.

      a new story begins.

WHAT ELSE DO WE BURN

it was december

for Sandra Quandelacy

it was december when you first saw them. they were singing. they
have been singing ever since. inside you, outside you. you
hear them in your blood. you hear them in your breathing. you
hear them in your flesh. they have sunk into your bones and
swim in your marrow. dragonflies and stars.

he reads you the stories. every single hair on your body is
standing. you see nothing. only the river and the night sky. you
see her rounded mouth. there are voices. you don't know the
words but what are words when the quiet things are singing.
what is the world when everything is singing.

you know that was the moment. you were dying before that
moment. you would have died without that moment. sometimes
your life depends on a photo. a carving. a story. a song. many
songs.

your eyes touched their fused bodies. that embrace of the same
origin. you drowned in the heady scent of sweet corn warmed
by the sun. you ran your fingers lightly over the rounded
shapes you would recognize as corn even in your sleep.

it wasn't that the singing began again that night. it's that you
were able to hear it again. and that blood rushed through you
again. and that your heart ceased its silence. its stillness. and
there you were again. no longer lost. there you were. singing.

33

the geo-physics of de-tribalization

table of contents

Chapter 6. *Earthquakes:*
vehement earth, injured earth, ruptured
earth, lands come undone, millions disappeared,
nations forced from their lands, nations scattered
even the clouds wept

Chapter 7. *Floods:*
raging waters of amnesia which ripped away
all of our stories, leaving families, communities, nations
like broken-limbed debris

Chapter 8. *Sinkholes*:
erosion of our names and our languages,
cataclysms of forgetting, shadowed caves of shame, collapses which
rendered us unrecognizable

Chapter 9. *Magnetic fields:*
we are the children, electric in our waiting,
inexorably pulling us to each other, recognizing
no distinctions in time

Chapter 10. *Deep ocean currents:*
under the surface of the ocean, hidden and immense,
returning, rising, writing our names on the sand
we may be de-tribalized but we are still indigenous to this land

let us be the altars

for Natalia Sylvester

i don't need for my flesh to continue   let all the chaotic
madness of my blood rest after me   i am content
to think i will be remembered for my love and for my ords
          for as long as anyone chooses to remember me   i
won't need any altars   lit candles   marigolds   my
favorite foods   or my thousand beloved songs   when
i am gone   there will be no use in invoking me   my
spirit will not linger   and whatever of me moves on   will
no longer know its name   will not even understand what a
name is

my mother mourned her dead quietly   my father's people
didn't believe in those   cosas de indios he said   the
dead were dead   my mother kept a single plate with a small
candle burning for each loved lost one   candles that burned
for exactly one night   she remembered the 2nd of november's of
her childhood   spent in Texas camposantos   adorning
graves with marigolds   the women laying out feasts on
banquet tables   listening to songs and stories through the
night   waiting till dawn to eat   only after the ancestors
had had their fill

my youngest brother   my adopted son   was born on
the day of the dead   hummingbird man   fiercest warrior i
have ever known   he survived his first death in the womb
and was born humming   some lives hold more pain than can
          be comprehended   was his unflesh'd spirit   even
then   willing to bear some of the pain   destined for weaker
beings   so that they would not break   i've lost
count of how many deaths his spirit has survived

each return   each day   each moment   he cleaves
to beauty   creates it   believes in it   nurtures it
shares it   gives it   his life
two thousand miles from home   i learned how to build altars

for the dead   eighteen years old   my first deliberate altar
a place for all of my dead that i could name   i inherited
almost no photos   i inherited almost no names   i
wrote the names i knew on slips of paper   struck a match
for the candles   at eighteen there weren't very any   twenty
five years later   any true altar would resemble a bonfire
and twenty five years later   i accept neither the necessity of
photos or names   conquest and history and poverty and
migrations and shame   have taken burnt erased destroyed
what i would need to present   the orderly branches
of my ancestors

i was not meant to survive   we were not meant to survive
we were meant to be forgotten   obliterated   lost   until
one day our ancestors   our indigenous ancestors   could
be rendered myth   until the blood   still coursing in our
veins   could be denied   but we   stubborn we
refuse to forget   with names or without names   we light
the flames and sing the songs and tell the stories   fragmented
as they may be   what names do we need to know
we belong   what names do we need to know they belong to us

we weep and we weep   too many ancestors in unmarked
graves   too many grandmothers and grandfathers   too
many cousins sisters brothers children   even now they are
still dying   with and without names   and a million
marigolds are insufficient   so let us be the altars then   our
flesh and our eyes   and what we make with our hands   and

37

speak with our mouths   having carved words from our hearts
let our art be flame   and flower   and feast   for all our
ancestors   for all our kin   for all our dead

october 12, 2013

521 years still mourning the losses still carrying the scars
under our skin   pain that pricks that writhes that pierces
we remember with hollowed eyes   mourn what we do not even know
mourn losses too immense for names   collapsing in fits
with weeping and wailing   butchered hair scattered on the
ground   give me smoke for my hands   ashes for my skin   flames
for my eyes   something more than loss should name us kin
something   more than the land riven   wounded bloody
something more   than flags   or their absence   speak to me in the
language of the sky   so that   we recognize one another   weep
with me   remember with me   one year   or five centuries
always   we are   still mourning

after the third time the would-be burglar climbed into my 2nd floor patio and tried the doors

it is night it is dark here I am in the shadows where I cannot be seenfrom the ground long-bladed machete in hand I am waiting for those hands those fingers to grasp at the railing as he hoists his weight up and over then quick quick I will collect my due of blood and scream I am waiting and as I wait it comes to me that I am weary of tears that we are all weary of tears that my ancestors and my descendants are weeping and I can hear them weeping and I can taste their tears and this is what we have done and what we have done and what we have done until we are sick with grieving what has been taken what is being taken and what will be taken I am weary of tears I want blood I want an infinite machete extending all directions in time no one will touch my children or my ancestors with violence their blood will never be spilled will never have been spilt will not be spilling no dying now or then or to come no violence no injury no hurt no woman no child no man no person forced against their will no patch of earth or water or sky violated or polluted never violated in the time to come or the time that has passed my infinite machete swung by my infinite strength I will make a thousand layered necklace of severed hands to rest on my infinite chest let the fingers and limbs pile up in my wake I am weary of tears I am weary of grieving they will not touch what is not theirs they will not touch what is not theirs the earth is screaming and singing through me through me unleashed I will collect my due of blood and scream they will not touch what is not theirs they will not touch what is not theirs I will take their hands their fingers their hearts for wanting for having wanted what is not theirs not theirs not theirs not theirs not theirs not theirs these bodies these histories these dreams these families these lands these skies these nations these people these freedoms they are not theirs to take

prayer for the lost children

"Federal Agencies Lost Track of Nearly 1,500 (Im)Migrant Children Placed With Sponsors," NY Times, April 26, 2018

little ones, you cross my mind every day.

everyday i wish there were things i didn't know about this world. things i didn't understand about power and greed and lust and hate. things i have seen about pain and abuse and anguish and death. my heart knows some of them are already dead. knows some of them are living eternities of rape and hurt. my heart knows their mothers' tears have reason to never end. my heart knows some of them will never see their families again. at some point, they will forget their father's voice, their mother's embrace. some of them will lose their names, their histories, the lands that saw them born.

little ones, i hold you in my hands.

it is my country that has done this. my country and my not country. the country i was born to, the country i am a citizen of, the country that shamed and dispossessed and saw to the poverty and death of my ancestors. the country that in its greed and lust for power created the chaos and poverty in the children's countries of birth and forced them to seek life here. this my country that i am sworn to change, my soul pitted against its chant of greed greed greed and hate hate hate. but nothing i do will be in time for the lost children. as nothing i can do can change the fates of all the children lost in this my country's history. what we do from here is to recover what we can. to save who we can. to battle those who would feed the monster that demands more children lost.

little ones, my tears are flecked with blood for you.

i wanted to find the words to pray for you, little ones. but neither my tongue nor my heart are capable of pretending. i cannot will ignorance for myself. you live in me. and i am commanded to pray for you. a las diosas or to god or to the universe or to whatever deities have the power of mercy. to them i pray for you. if you are dead, i pray for peace for the infinite souls fled from your small bodies. if you are hurting, i pray for the end of that pain. if you are hungry, i pray for your sustenance. if you are cold, i pray for warmth. if you are inconsolable, i pray for your comfort. if you are weary, i pray for your rest. little ones, i send you love and strength. may the despair in my heart transform itself into light to cover you, to shield you, to feed you, to make you strong. may las diosas or god or the universe have mercy on you, hold you, and keep you. may you make a life for yourself one day that will allow you to heal, allow you to find peace, allow you to love, allow you to live as you choose.

forgive me, little ones, that this is all i can do.

a song of burning

i never forget the ash a thousand thousand black wings in the sky
black against a blue so blue so wide so bright
                                        i'd see the ash and
know they were setting fire to the sugar cane fields before harvest
burning away leaves and straw and tops
                                clearing and cleaning
causing the creatures to flee the scorpions the snakes the bees
rendering it safe for the workers to collect the precious stalks
                                        what else do we burn
with this purpose this desire to shed the unnecessary to concentrate
one single intent to collect the sweet
                        what else do we burn
knowing we are not destroying not erasing only doing away with
the chaff and husk of us the mean the petty the unjust
                                have you
never heard the fire singing singing as if every sound hurt as if
every note was pulled from deep within and the leap from emotion
to sound left a wound
                        ragged and bleeding but give me that song it
is the song i need to stay true the fire has come the fire has sung
                                                        i
am straight blackened stalks of cane now bare to the eyes bare to
the hands
    only the sweet of me left and i obey my gods speak when
they bid me speak set myself on fire when they say it is time for
harvest
    some sweet is the collected essence of flowers some sweet
grows long and green swaying with the wind under the sun until it
is brought forth from flame and ash

43

                    and i am ash always the ash
in the sky and i am the sky and the light landing on the black of my
ash

     and when my gods bid me rise again i rise again and i will
rise again whenever they bid me until there is nothing left with
which to rise

marrow and light

            she did not know the
name of the earth she walked on she did not
know the name of the sky she walked under
did not know the name of the sun or the
name of the moon did not know the name of
the rain that fell on her body she did not
know the name of her spirit she did not
know her name or her mother's name or her
mother's mothers' names

            but when she cried
out to the thunder whose name she did not
know and when she cried out to the sky and
the rain and the pink light of dawn whose
names she did not know she ripped two
languages out of her mouth both tongues
aflame in her hands both tongues fluttering
into a cloud of black ash around her

            when she made
sounds that were not recognizable words and
were not names when she made sounds
created by the marrow in her bones and the
light that fell out of her eyes when she spoke
with her new tongue this third tongue still
only a raw nub unable to shape sound

            when she cried out of
need distilling longing into song the thunder
answered the sun answered the moon and
the sky the earth answered

        and then what she did
not know did not matter not the names that
had been lost not the names that had been
taken abandoned names starved names
disappeared names
buried names no names

          what mattered
was that her soul with its lost name had always
lived in this third tongue what mattered was
that not everything had been lost the world
spoke in marrow and light light and marrow

THE SOUL SPEAKS A LANGUAGE OF LIGHT

roadtripping with Cipactli

feed me wildflowers feed me road feed me sky, you say, your crocodile
mouth shaping each word strangely but ecstatically. *fill my eyes
my mouth my hands all of me,* you say, your crocodile hand with its
webbed fingers trying to catch the wind. we drive over a bridge,
the air changing slightly. you lean back in your seat, closing your
eyes, taking in the sensation. we drive, for miles and miles, south
and further south. no houses, no towns, only mesquites and nopales
and more mesquites.

you're always hungry. we stop for burgers in carrizo springs. we
use the drive-thru. you eat yours all the way with bacon and cheese
and jalapenos. we feed chicken tenders to all your other mouths.
one of them has a sweet tooth and wants ice cream. we feed it an
apple pie. i might be getting too comfortable with you in the car. i
almost lose a finger.

we don't stay there for long. someone might have seen you. i
keep checking the rearview mirror. no sign of Tezcatlipoca or
Quetzalcoatl. still, it doesn't hurt to be cautious. i decide it's time
to go east. highway 85. you don't say anything. you're too busy
working my phone, trying to choose what music you want to listen
to next.

in austin, you kept flipping back and forth between Willie Nelson
and Ruben Ramos. in san antonio, it was classic tejano with lots of
Selena and La Mafia and Mazz and Elsa Garcia and some Ram
Herrera. after uvalde, it was all Chente and Jose Alfredo and
Lucha and Chavela. finally, you put the phone down. there are
so few cars on the road i feel safe hitting 90 miles an hour. all of
the huge bugs we're killing with the windshield are dying to the
sounds of El General, Don Omar, and Ivy Queen.

i love the road, you exclaim, your body shivering from top to bottom. i just grin, showing all my teeth. *i know what you mean,* i say, *there's nothing like it.* i don't know where we're going. i didn't ask any questions when you showed up at my door and said, *i've got to get out of town.* i grabbed a change of clothes, some water, my bag, my keys. everything else was already in the car: serape, pillow, machete. the essentials. it was still dark when we left. in the still cool morning of spring.

i feel a sudden longing for the beach. i turn to look at you, wondering if that's what you need. the gulf. south padre's too crowded. but we could head towards port isabel, then take that one road that goes and goes, trees and grass giving way to sand dunes and open sky. i could take you there. you look at me suddenly, your eyes intent, your words low and careful. *i won't let them take me again. i'd rather die.* i don't say anything. just nod. i don't call you corazon out loud, but you know it's what i always mean when i look at you. not like i could talk around the knot in my throat anyway. but you understand. i won't leave you. freedom or death.

axolotl

little warrior
almost imperceptibly
scarred
from so much healing
how many regrown limbs
how many repaired organs
even precious
brain tissue
created anew

teach me this
little warrior
how you remain
tender and
infinite
soft and eternal
in the face of struggle
how it is the healing
has already begun
even before the wound

after The Sunflower (Gustav Klimt, 1907)

leaves. a multitude of green leaves. petals. a
multitude of golden petals. green life infused with
sunlight.

you stand out. loom large with your violet streaked
leaves. your sturdy stalk. your wide frame. your
bright mane.

though you are a flower, you are sometimes
repellant. your function of seed-making far
outweighing your allotment of petals.

sunflower, i am afraid we are too much alike. we
are not the rose, the lily, the glorious orchid. not
beautiful. we are driven to survive and make seed.

but, sunflower, we have been given a singular gift,
you and i — our faces follow the sun.

infinitive verb

here is the secret:
        we are choosing from infinity
              and we are free

for every wall

        every boundary
            every limit
                not of our choosing

we must again speak
        again practice
            again demand

the place within
        where infinity lives
            where we create

infinity whirling within
        i feed it
            it feeds me

do we need a name
        for the divine within
            the divine without

where we most
        are ourselves and where
                we cease to be

the infinitive form:
        to create —
            all i need as
                a name for god

Nagual: blood

Call the spirits. Call the hunger. Call the running. No moon here.
No light. No cities. All our names embedded along the long roads.
We have wept and bled here. Leaving fur. Leaving claws. Leaving
feathers. Leaving skin. Night is not the time for remembering.
Leave it to the morning. Leave it to the day. Darkness is for
breathing. Darkness is for pushing the thin membranes that
separate us from each other. From the earth. The air. The wind.
Night is for speaking what we fear in the daylight. Ending.
Becoming. Seeing. The trusting senses fall away and we fill with
the flowing surety of what we know without words. What we
wrote when language was symbol and color and image. When we
wrote everything in blood.

Nagual: smoke

Call the wings. Call the hollowed bones. Call the howling. Call the smoke. We need the smoke. Be born in smoke. Lose our edges. Our limits. Our endings and beginnings. Smoke in the wind. Call the flame. We need the flame. Without flame we forget. Without smoke we hold too tight to these upright shapes. These too solid shapes. This is not everything we are. In the ashing flesh we'll see the glimmering stars. Smoke limbs. Smoke running close to the ground. Smoke womb enveloping us in a language without words. In our mouths — tongues of smoke.

Nagual: rivers

Body of water. Body of light. Body of earth. The human shape forgets possible transformations. Forgets that it is only a shape. Leave it. Let it return to light. To rivers. A vessel to fill and empty. We are what always remains. With names. Without. With skin. Without. We are what changes. Not the story but what gives the stories life. We are what cannot be seen. Call the night. Call the stars. Call the wind. Call the earth. The earth will rise to meet us. The earth will lead us to the places where it cleaves. Apart and together. Where it changes. We are bodies of thunder. Bodies without time. Our bodies are rivers.

the scatterer of ashes

what does it mean
to be born of a cataclysm
there was one world
and then there was another
there is no known number
for five centuries of death

we are children of ash
children of fire
children of corpses
children of blood soaked earth
mourning all these centuries
because we cannot
lay all their spirits to rest

mourning because new blood
revives the cries of old blood
because new tears fall everyday
to join the rivers of old tears
flowing inside the earth

mourning because we have seen
too many of our own die
and the dying has not ended
we mourn the nameless future dead
as we mourn the nameless past dead

what offerings can we make to
Nextepuah
the scatterer of ashes
when so much
has already been sacrificed

been lost been taken

scatter the ashes
Nextepuah
and let them rest

what does it mean
to be born knowing
we are destined for ash

lay them to rest
Nextepuah
and in return we offer this
when it is time
to scatter our ashes
you will find only
flames flickering
over our stubborn hearts

because we are not ash
we are neither dead
nor dying
not today
for all our dead
we will live
incandescent

we are children of survive
children of struggle
children of sing
children of pray
children of resist
five centuries of dying
has also been five centuries

— of living of remembering
— of gathering of building
— of stories of birthing

Nextepuah
we may weep but
even our ashes will sing

the story we heard at dawn

from their first breath, the wanderers had known their fate. some rebelled and chose the cliffs, the dark river, the knife. some had families and lived each given day loving them. some set themselves on the road early, wanting to drink in the world, gather all its stories.

but for each of them came a morning, a morning before the night could even begin to blue, that brought the whoo of an owl. they may have cried out. they may have bowed their heads. they may have wept. they may have danced. when the sun rose, all their bodies rose in response.

they embraced their loved ones. left their homelands. left every possession abandoned on the road.

the wanderers came from the east, from the south, from the west, from the north. some journeyed for days, some journeyed for years. when they met at the appointed place, they recognized one another. dark, dark their skin. red, red their hearts. gold, gold their eyes.

touching fingers, they stood shoulder to shoulder. faced the east. with a sigh, their feet sank into the earth, tendons stretching and rooting. their torsos thinned and paled. their arms, held up to the sky, greened into the falling arcs of leaves. their faces, joyous and weary and intent on the sun, became tender golden kernels. their tears and their laughter streamed down in white tassels.

this is how corn came to be.

let the dawn break

slowly softly brightly

over your skin

let the darkness

subside tenderly

even the piercing

memories of stars

growing hazy now

night will come again

night always comes again

wake gently

wake carefully

this day is not for weeping

your heart says

this day is not for raging

there are days

meant for surrender and rest

and growing strong

touch the earth with bare feet

feet that have run worked hurt

today let them touch the earth

gently rhythmically

hold your own shoulders

so accustomed to burdens

to bracing against blows

hold them like blossoms

precious and many-petaled

release your waist your hips

the spaces between

repositories of so much pain

yours and what was inherited

and the pain of those you love

let your body sway

hips weeping hips laughing

hips affirming that

life is still sweet

life is still

life is

repeat this

caressing your own lips

so that you remember

you are your own sun

let us become want

become hunger with me become whole with me set flame to what was extinguished i am and am not speaking of bodies but i am always speaking intangible interior indefinable

our histories of famine teach us silence if we give it no words the hurt doesn't exist and all the limits all the walls teach us to throttle our half-formed dreams

in the difficult years there isn't enough fuel to keep the light of what we are burning in the difficult years everyone else comes first in the difficult years we endure endure endure

our lights dim we become dangers to ourselves gnawing through our own hands our hands covering our own mouths keeping us from speaking denying us sustenance

but the soul is all hunger all want all desire the soul speaks a language of light a language of crave touch bite be burn a language of flame to create is a fire to heal is a fire to live is a fire

let us live let us become want let us become everything that is bright everything that speaks everything that dreams everything that reaches become hunger with me

if you are hungry, i will feed you

from *A Little Chaos* (2014)

my pantries are full   bursting with preserves
       dried herbs   salted meats
    my gardens lush   with salad greens
the bursting   rounded bodies   of tomatoes
       zucchinis   eggplants
    my orchards sighing   with branches
low and heavy   with fruit sweet
       and incandescent
   all lying in wait   for so long too long
    eons   suns and moons   moons
and moons   seasons years and years
    there is such   hunger in you
       it inspires an ache   in me

    bite my hands   when i bring
    golden fruit   to your lips
    slip my hair   into your mouth
    and sigh   when you release it
   all of this   my arms my breasts
my belly my thighs   my limbs my skin
offered up to yours   let there be nothing
left unassuaged   unmet   unsaid
    no appetite   unsatisfied
i would see you slaked   sleek soothed
let me   erase the gauntness of your cheeks
   the bottomless   longing in your eyes

    when i   was young   i tore
out my heart   burned it   ashed it
so i could breathe   the second heart
wore itself out   bittered and starved

it didn't   even whimper
and i became   accustomed to its absence
but this third one   sprouted unlooked for
ate the rain and the sun and the breeze
flowered fruited   and now red fleshed
it has no bruise   no mark
no hurt no scar   this one has no fear
it gives   and gives   never depleting

if you are hungry i will feed you

the earth of us

for Rosemary Catacalos

"nosotras mismas somos la tierra nueva y lista para sembrar"
—Rosemary Catacalos

into the flesh of us
lavender and jasmine
and the stuff of stars

almas mias
this is the work of our lives
the black earth of us
wet with tears and sweat
and the sex of us
composted with our dreams
and our tragedies

sunlight and moonlight
limning the bone
marrow blood flesh skin of us
all our words the knives
for peeling away at
the disordered delicate
dangerous disturbed of us
until light falls unfettered
out of our eyes
the spoken the prayed
the love in the hands of us

seeds breaking open
in the revolving regenerating
rising intensity of us
and the sought for healing

stronger and stronger
streaming out of our chests
in the expanding suns of us

at our end there will be
only one essential story

what we made of the earth of us

devotional

i am a lit fire
burning nothing
around me

my eyes
are smoke

from my head
not a torrent of serpents
but a torrent
of lions' mouths

lions' roars
in my eyes

in me
all fire
wrought into
bells and flowers
bows and arrows

no division
no separation
pure longing

all of my limbs
are animals now

warning for the young wanting to heal generations past

you will want to envision entire valleys filled with benevolent
ancestors will want to shower them with spring rain and
multicolored blossoms and speak to the wind and the rivers and
endlessly braid the sweetgrass as you call their names known and
not known but do not forget

our ghosts have teeth our ghosts died sick died mad died cursing
their killers cursing their children died stabbed died shot died
starving died alone died abandoned died hopeless died watching
their people die with them died watching their homes burnt to the
ground died watching their crops destroyed died in boarding
schools died in catholic missions died in battle died in the cold of
cities died crossing rivers died in prisons died sick died diseased
died forgotten

death does not remove despair
death does not remove rage
death does not restore everything

our ghosts have teeth centuries of ghosts with teeth are our
birthright as much as the wisdom and endurance of ancestors we
are born with teeth we can't always wield wisely we are born with
the desire to rend ourselves the desire to rip each other apart we are
born with teeth that lust for the shudder of flesh

in the long work of healing we must hold our eyes open speak also
to the destruction within must hold close our ghosts with teeth
must learn our teeth use them to free ourselves and each other use
them to rip the seams of time and hurt and loss use them to tear
open the festering wounds we must learn to use our teeth as tools
not weapons

CUICACALLI

cuicacalli

i. body of song

never say we did not speak.

our tongue is an infinite tongue.
strong in its ignorance of your
american time. its roots reaching
deep into the earth where sunlight
and the memory of sunlight live in
the darkness. there are songs
breathing in our words. there are
songs breathing in the sunlight. there
are songs breathing in the earth.

our hands are breathing with songs.

we are inhabitants of a border
inhabited by a border. we say
tejanos. we say mexicanos. we say
mexicans from this side. mexicans
from that side. we say mexican
americans. we say chicanos, xicanos,
xicanxs. we say tex mex. we say
indigenous. some of us know the
names. Kickapoo. Apache.
Comanche. some of us know. many
do not. but we know. we know. we
say here. we say there. we say there
is no line. we say. we say. we mean
us the people. we mean we who
belong to this land. to all our lands.

we mean we. our hands working this
soil. we mean we. our feet dancing
on this earth. we keeping it turning.
we mean we. our blood spilled here.

we mean we. equal parts earth and
sun.

ii. earth of song

February 2, 1848 — Treaty of
Guadalupe Hidalgo

we are the lost children of a broken
treaty. the dispossessed though the
ink provided for the protection of
persons and property. is it a treaty
when one side never intended to
honor it. when the ink itself was
greed made manifest.

we are the many times dispossessed.

Land of the Alabama. Land of the
Apache. Land of the Aranama. Land
of the Atakapan. Land of the Bidai.
Land of the Caddo. Land of the
Comanche. Land of the Choctaw.
Land of the Coushatta. Land of the
Hasinai. Land of the Jumano. Land
of the Karankawa. Land of the
Kickapoo. Land of the Kiowa. Land

of the Tonkawa. Land of the
Wichita.

we claim all of our blood. all of this
land. all of these americas.

though we were dispossessed when
the spanish came. dispossessed when
the mexican shamed the indigenous
of us. dispossessed when the whites
came as immigrants to texas which
was still mexico. dispossessed when
they fought mexico in order to
preserve slavery.

dispossessed when the united states
said manifest destiny.

in school we are taught manifest
destiny as if it was everything—
doctrine and driving need.
inescapable destiny. the happy ever
after. but remember always
remember though our history may be
written in blood — what they teach us
is only the slightest sliver of the
truth. not everyone believed in the
necessity of a western coast. the
necessity of war. the necessity of
dispossession. the necessity of death.
and always always there are those
who resist.

iii. blood of song

we do not forget to sing.

we sing when we are screaming. we
sing when we are whispering. we
sing when we are praying. we sing
when we are dying. this is what my
blood knows. my ancestors have
sung unceasingly.

they still sing.

they translate the matanza of 1915 as
a massacre but matanza is more
accurately translated as slaughter. as
in the slaughter of animals. the treaty
of 1848 ended the mexican american
war they say but the war on
mexicans on mexican americans
never ended. decades upon decades
of our people killed in plain sight.
killed with impunity. bodies hung
from trees. bodies collapsed on the
ground. bodies left to rot. some of
the killers were vigilantes. some of
the killers were eager to steal the
land steal the land steal the land. if
the history books admit to 187,000
acres of land taken in this time in
south texas alone how many acres do
we imagine were lost in reality.

some of the killers were texas
rangers.

the history books use careful
language. say there were 'excesses'
of force but even they will admit the
rangers were created with the intent
to kill mexicans. mexicans on both
sides of the river. created with the
intent to kill native americans. they
saw our people as animals to
slaughter and they slaughtered them
and they slaughtered them.
thousands and thousands from 1915
to 1919 alone.

a bitter thing to see brown-skinned
children playing pretending to be
texas rangers.

the slaughtered are still singing. there
is a song only spilled blood sings.
one part lamentation. one part
prayer. one part rage. one part
creation. one part fractured into
nameless parts.

iv. memory of song

No dogs or Mexicans Allowed.

No dogs, no Negroes, no Mexicans
Allowed.

We serve Whites only, no Mexicans
or Spanish.

my mother was born in 1940. had a
first grade education but she could
read those signs. she remembered
those signs. and all the places where
those signs were not necessary
because she knew she was not
welcome. in this land of segregated
schools. segregated wealth.
segregated neighborhoods.
segregated graveyards.

when my mother told me her first
memories of language she told me
about learning to sign her name. how
at least she didn't have to sign with
an x. and she told me about those
signs.

my mother died in 2001. all her life
it seemed she never entered any
space without looking for the signs
explicit or intangible that would say
she was not welcome.

all her life, she never assumed safety.
never assumed protection.

v. people of song

what is a border. what is a nation.
what are citizens. what is north. what
is south. what is a people.

blood recognizes blood.

lines on a map are not real. history is
a story told and told crooked. nations
are a falsehood.

until they are not. until the lines are
used to dispossess. to rip. to tear. to
say these families have no right to be
together. this person has no right to
their land. this person is no longer a
citizen. no longer legal. no longer
human.

because only humans have rights.

what was repatriation but another
way to break the treaty. what was
repatriation but another way to steal
land. another way to render us not-
human.

400,000 to 2 million mexicans and
americans of mexican descent
deported to mexico in seven years.
citizenship did not matter. 60 percent
of them were born citizens and were

still deported. it was their names
their skin that made them targets.

they did not use the phrase ethnic
cleansing then.

but what else can you call it.

then and now.

vi. bones of song

you ask if the bones are heavy. bones
are always heavy.

they bear the weight of a life. the
weight of all the lives that came
before them and the lives that
followed. they bear the weight of
blood and muscle and sinew. of grief
and work and loss and time.

Falfurrias, Brooks County, Texas

the words 'mass' and 'grave' live in
the nebulous place where we put all
the words we must keep at a distance
so that we can breathe. and sleep.
and live. so that we can work. so that
we can hope. the distance at which
you keep nightmares. the distance at
which you keep history. the distance

at which you keep the stories that all
these words invoke:
lynching.
traincar.
texas ranger.
separation.
repatriation.
border wall.
death.
murder.
death.
murder.
death.

and the word that is poison:
forget.

if remembering was not important,
the bones would not remain. bones
would rot and fall away like flesh.
bones would liquefy dry and flake
away. bones would be the
consistency of flower petals and
dragonfly wings. bones would bear
no stories no names. bear no essence.
bones would bend and sway as
inconsequential things do.

they didn't come here to die.

they came looking for work for the
end of violence for life for family for
dreams.

they didn't come here to die.

how many other deaths in the desert.
there are bones from the gulf of
mexico to the pacific ocean. when
there is dust you must ask yourself
how much of it is bone. how much of
it is anguish. how much of it is now
nameless.

they said. enforcement through
deterrence. they said it. they say it
again. they are saying it now. let
them risk their lives. let them lose
everything. and when they are
nothing bury them like animals.

because they dare to cross a line.

in falfurrias. little town so close to
the border. little town with its name
of uncertain origin. lipan. spanish.
french. bastard name for a little town
that might as well be named
checkpoint. checkpoint texas. little
town where brown people live and
brown people die. many brown
people die. what else do mass graves
signify.

what mass graves always signify.

these

are not humans. mass graves with
bodies in trash bags. mass graves
with skulls and bones all tossed in
together. names are lost in mass
graves. and many someones are still
praying for the safety of their father
mother son daughter wife husband
child child child but they are praying
for bones.

nothing but bones.

sometimes it seems the border is a
graveyard. soaked with blood. all the
bones beneath the ground rattling
rattling. but remember the border is
not a line. the border extends
hundreds of miles both south and
north and even further. the border is
everywhere there are bodies. and
bones. the border is everywhere we
die because of lines on a map.

El Paso/Juarez

we will say femicides. we will say
border and mean a narrow strip of
land. we will say border and think of
the women who have marked their
panties with blood. women who
cross with morning after pills
because they know they will be
raped. women on both sides dying.

women on both sides killed. we will
say femicides and think border but
indigenous women across these
continents are missing are taken are
killed. bodies abandoned. women
killed and no one names the killers.
women killed and women killed and
women killed and when will it end.
women being killed. women
being taken and women being killed.

voices whisper from all their bones.

vii. breath of song

in the beginning, before the first
word, there was a breath. and an
infinite moment of decision. to
whisper. to scream. to speak. to sing.
or perhaps there was no such
moment. perhaps there was no doubt.
perhaps there was only ever one
choice.

because the first breath was created
for song.

because we were created for song.

so let us be song. shaped by song and
shapers of song. carriers and keepers.
inheritors and creators.

let us be song.

viii. house of song

if i sing you songs, will you listen.

i am a house of song. you are a house
of song. we are a house of song.
however we began wherever we
began however and wherever we
end. whatever we might have been or
could still yet be. we are a house of
song.

rage and love intermingled in us.
and only the song to keep us name us
make us heal us remember us whole.
the song the house the place where
grief and tenderness sleep. where
remembering wakes and daydreams.
wakes and daydreams. the place
where the daily choice to sing is
made. is lit and set alight.

this is the house where we sleep and
then wake to stare at the sun
and pace the earth and chant, we survive,
we survive, we survive. and by
chanting we live. by chanting we do
not forget. we sing. we wail. we pour
ourselves out of our mouths until

'sing' and 'wail' are not distinct
things. until singing is wailing and
wailing is singing.

the land sings us. sings us until we
are and are not the history. until we
are and are not the bodies. until we
are and are not the dispossessed.
until we are and are not the hunted
the rejected the repatriated the
violated the lost.

the land sings us so that we do not
surrender.

not then. not now. not ever. not in
this time or that time. not in this time
of lost children. not in this time of
walls.

we cede nothing. forget nothing. the
voices are here. the voices are with
us. within us.

the voices do not end. the singing
does not end. the voices sing and the
voices sing and the voices sing and if
you hear silence it is only because all
the voices have become one.
sometimes it will seem as if you are
hearing silence but what you are
hearing is the singing of all the
voices in the universe singing at once
with one unending breath the voices
do not end the singing does not end
and the voices sing and the voices

sing though bodies may suffer and
bodies may die the stories do not end
the song does not end this is a house
of song and in this house of song
singing does not end the singing does
not end the singing does not end the
singing does not end the singing does
not end the singing does not end the
singing does not end the song never
ends

AFTERWORD

Nomiccāmā Nomiccānacayo and the Necessity of Art in Difficult Times

I was invited in October 2017 to deliver the keynote for a Chicana Arts and Activism Symposium in Topeka, Kansas — organized and hosted by Christina Valdivia-Alcala, the Tonantzin Society, and Mulvane Museum at Washburn University. Their theme was "Art and Resistance in the Age of Extremism." I wanted to write something that would speak to the despair — the faltering faith — of many artists and activists around me, something that would remind us all why our art is necessary and how it helps to sustain our communities. I shared this piece with La Voz because I have found myself wanting to share this keynote with many friends. I offer it here in the hopes that it serves as a reminder of why we must continue our work and how we can help strengthen our hearts, as individuals and as a community.

Para servirles,

ire'ne lara silva

Keynote delivered October 13, 2017 at the Midwest Chicana Arts & Activism Symposium

Mil gracias to the Tonantzin Society, Christina Valdivia-Alcala, the Mulvane Art Museum, and Washburn University for the invitation to speak today. I would like to share some thoughts that have been in my head and my heart over the last year.

I woke up weeping on November 9, 2016. And though I went to work and answered the phone and wrote emails and did all the other tasks that encompass my workday, I never stopped weeping. Not that day or the next or the next. With growing horror, I heard about the rising tide of hate crimes sweeping across our country. Over the next few months, I felt paralysis and despair warring with protest and a deep, deep seated rage.

It both comforted me and inspired awe to see people pouring into the streets and marching by the dozens, hundreds, thousands, millions. I had a small hope that flickered, that said, this could not be. Inauguration Day will not come. And then it did. I felt it like a blow to my stomach and not just mine but to our collective stomach. None of us could breathe.

In the last nine months, there has been no end to the battering: the repeated assaults on the Affordable Care Act and women's rights, police violence, Charlottesville, the increased presence of Neo-Nazis and white supremacists, the building of the wall, anti-immigrant hostility, ICE raids, mass deportations, the attacks on DACA, the dismantling of environmental protections, the undermining of our educational system, the crisis in Puerto Rico, the ongoing violations of Indigenous rights, and the imminent threat of war. The battering is emotional, psychological, spiritual, and very, very physical with real threats to our well-being and to that of our families, loved ones, neighbors, communities, to our world itself.

It is a wonder that we can breathe at all.

94

The end of 2016 and the beginning of 2017 were difficult, but on that most difficult day in January something in me rallied. Those of you who know me, know that I live on Facebook, and that was where I posted my first thoughts that were not full of despair:

Don't drink the poison, my people. Don't breathe it. Don't let in to your bodies, your minds, or your spirits. This is a long work we have coming. And we must be strong and outlast them all. Breathe the clean air and look up to the sky and hold each other up. Don't let them drown out the songs. Let the singing unfurl, let it wave in the wind, let it cast lightning, let it loose in your blood, let the singing loose from your eyes and your hands.

Because, I thought, none of this is going to rob me of myself or make me less of who I am. None of this is going to stop me from doing my work or manifesting my vision. None of this is going to make me give up, give in, surrender. None of this is going to render me meat for despair or apathy or neglect or rage or exhaustion.

In times like these, there are certain questions that we must ask ourselves and then definitively answer or re-affirm so that we can continue our work. How do we go on? What do activism and art mean in our lives? Who are we without them? What do we owe to ourselves, our communities, our ancestors?

The first temptation is to believe that art is meaningless, that our poems and paintings and music mean nothing in the face of hate, violence, and unjust laws. To believe that time spent in creation, in contemplation, is time that could be better spent doing something — anything — else.

But to believe these things is to surrender the greatest part of what we are, to hand over our hearts — still red and beating — on a platter to those who already threaten to take so much from us — it is to hand over our hearts before they even think to come for them.

I will not surrender my heart. I will not surrender my art. My poems and my stories are what I have to give in this world. What

I give I give in the hope that it will sustain and inspire the work of artists, activists, and cultural workers — as their work sustains and inspires me. As great or as humble as my offerings may be, what I know is that what is offered in love feeds us all. It is no accident that culture, art, and activism keep intersecting, time and time again, because each one feeds the other, because it keeps us connected so that even the rage and grief we feel are rage and grief rooted in love. Love for ourselves. Love for our families. Love for our communities. Love for our people. Love for our shared humanity.

Our task is to remain human. To become neither monsters nor victims. What we owe the ancestors: to live to love to create to dream to fight to act to speak to learn to teach to grieve. As they survived to love to create to dream to fight to act to speak to learn to teach to grieve. To one day become ancestors ourselves and inspire those who will follow. What is owed to the ancestors: We remain strong. We refuse to surrender. We give them no victims. We remain human. We dedicate ourselves this day and every day to the work we have chosen, to the work which has chosen us.

And to do this — we must not drink the poison. While our culture possesses the concepts of limpias and barridas — of cleansing and detoxifying, of healing — it exacts a heavy toll on us, this cycle of wounding and healing, of poisoning and detoxifying.

We have to find another way. We must become the curators of our emotions, our minds, our spirits. And if 'to curate' seems a strange concept, remember that the word 'curate' read in Spanish is curate — 'heal yourself'…in this case, 'heal yourself before the wound.'

It has been my thinking that as artists, we choose what influences us, what affects us. That this is how we develop our voices, our visions, our practices. An artist's development, an artist's inspiration is often spoken of as if the artist is a passive recipient, tossed and turned this way and that way. But I don't think this is true. An artist is the curator of their own creativity, selecting and featuring the elements that shape them and their work.

The practice of curating is no different for activists, as they choose where to channel their energy and their passion, as they choose to become educators or organizers or protestors or social workers or legislators or even, writers. As they choose, day in and day out, to believe that change is possible, that affecting even a single human life is worth their labor. As they choose to act, remembering relentlessly, that their actions are not fueled by rage but by love.

In my life, I have been cast, again and again, into the role of caregiver — in medical crises that have gone on, day after day, week after week, month after month, year after year. And while you pray for the best and prepare for the worst, what you come to learn is a different kind of strength. At first, you hold all the fear and worry inside and wait to weep until no one is leaning on you and no one can see you. And then perhaps you learn to bottle it all inside until you live with a hard knot in your stomach and a hard fist around your heart. But eventually, neither the wild weeping nor the hard knot nor the hard fist are sustainable. Instead, you train yourself. Every day, you train yourself not to admit in fear and worry. You train yourself to keep your eyes open and your heart soft and your hands ready and strong.

As artists and activists, we can train ourselves to keep our eyes open and our hearts soft. To curate what we allow in, what work we choose, in what spirit we do that work. We can choose not to drink the poison.

I contacted my friend, the poet/writer/translator David Bowles, to help me with this concept I had no name for. English seemed insufficient to the task. I couldn't think of anything in Spanish that wasn't about a limpia or barrida — a way of cleansing or purifying after the fact, after the harm. Nothing for how to keep the harm from being inflicted in the first place. What I wanted was something that would name the act of protecting ourselves against poison, of becoming so strong that we would not let ourselves be injured. And it came to me that I needed a name in Nahuatl.

David suggested something but said that it was perhaps a little too dark, that it was a phrase than translated literally as "dead hands, dead flesh" but meant "protected by supernatural forces." It seemed intriguing but a bit strange. Until he told me the next part — that "dead hands, dead flesh" might more accurately mean to be protected by the "hands and bodies of my departed loved ones."

I read those words as if lightning had flashed into my eyes, and every hair on my body stood up. Nomiccāmā Nomiccānacayo is to say, I am protected by my ancestors, by the bodies of my departed loved ones, by all of the power and life they represent. This is how I want to walk this earth. Surrounded by that love, protected by that strength, made wise by their endurance, made brave by their example. I want to cultivate in myself the wisdom to know what I should allow in — what will strengthen me, sustain me, inspire me, teach me — and what I should perceive as poison and turn away — everything that would cast me into the role of monster or victim, what would make me calloused or apathetic, despairing or weak.

I want to be a part of a strong community — artists, activists, and cultural workers — and to live in a space marked by their brilliance and their passion.

Nomiccāmā Nomiccānacayo. I am protected. Tomiccāmā Tomiccānacayo. We are protected.

Acknowledgments

With grateful acknowledgment for the journals and anthologies where these poems first appeared:

"geo-physics of de-tribalization" in *Kuikatl;* "october 12, 2013" in *Dialogo;* "what i remembered yesterday", "nagual: blood, nagual: smoke, nagual: rivers," "prayer for the lost children", and "poem for Tlatecuhtli" in *Acentos;* "a song for burning" in *Jet Fuel Review;* "Coatlicue" in *Woman Poets Across the Americas;*

With grateful acknowledgment to the 2017 NALAC Fund for the Arts Grant that gave me time and resources to create this work.

And many thanks to poet/author David Bowles for his invaluable expertise and willingness to answer my endless questions.

About the Author

ire'ne lara silva is the author of two poetry collections, *furia* (Mouthfeel Press, 2010) and *Blood Sugar Canto* (Saddle Road Press, 2016), which were both finalists for the International Latino Book Award in Poetry, an e-chapbook, *Enduring Azucares*, (Sibling Rivalry

Press, 2015), as well as a short story collection, *flesh to bone* (Aunt Lute Books, 2013) which won the Premio Aztlán. She and poet Dan Vera are also the co-editors of *Imaniman: Poets Writing in the Anzaldúan Borderlands*, (Aunt Lute Books, 2017), a collection of poetry and essays.

ire'ne is the recipient of a 2017 NALAC Fund for the Arts Grant, the final recipient of the Alfredo Cisneros del Moral Award, the Fiction Finalist for AROHO's 2013 Gift of Freedom Award, and the 2008 recipient of the Gloria Anzaldúa Milagro Award.

ire'ne is currently working on her first novel, *Naci*.

Cuicacalli / House of Song is her newest collection of poetry.

her website is: irenelarasilva.wordpress.com

CPSIA information can be obtained
at www.ICGtesting.com
Printed in the USA
LVHW091647221220
674907LV00009B/1749